D0468505

Wind and Water at Work

A Book About Change

Thomas F. Sheehan

Rourke
Publishing LLC
Vero Beach, Florida 32964

www.rourkepublishing.com

PHOTO CREDITS: title page © Tore johannesen; P04a © Sonja; P04b © Sonja; P05 © Simon Krzic; P06 © Michael Rieger/FEMA; P07a © Losevsky Pavel; P07b © Gordana Sermek; P08 © Holger Wulschlaeger; P09 © James M. Phelps Jr.; P11 © Sonya Etchison; P12 © James M. Phelps Jr.; P13 © Pierdelune; P14 © Jhaz Photography; p14b © Kondrachov Vladimir; P16a © Stephanie Dankof; P16b © Tony Campbell; P17 © Bull's-Eye Arts; P18 © Andrea Booher/FEMA; P19 © Jocelyn Augustino/FEMA; P20 © Keith Levit; P21a © Damian P. Gadal; P21b © Photodisc, Inc.

Editor: Robert Stengard-Olliges

Cover design by Michelle Moore.

Library of Congress Cataloging-in-Publication Data

Sheehan, Thomas F., 1939-
Wind and water at work : a book about change / Thomas F. Sheehan.
p. cm. -- (Big ideas for young scientists)
ISBN 978-1-60044-538-5 (Hardcover)
ISBN 978-1-60044-699-3 (Softcover)
1. Wind power--Juvenile literature. 2. Wind power--Climatic factors--Juvenile literature. 3. Water-power--Juvenile literature. 4. Erosion--Juvenile literature. I. Title.
TJ820.S54 2008
551.3'5--dc22

2007019508

Printed in the USA

CG/CG

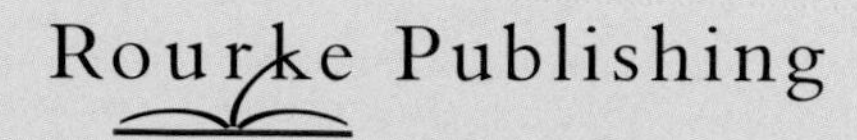

www.rourkepublishing.com – rourke@rourkepublishing.com
Post Office Box 3328, Vero Beach, FL 32964

Table of Contents

Earth Changes

You live on a planet that is always changing. On Earth, wind and moving water pick up all sorts of objects and fling them someplace else.

Of course, riding the wind and water can be lots of fun, too.

Water currents, large and small, can move objects along in a hurry, or slowly, over a long period of time.

Tornadoes and hurricane winds are powerful, but even a little breeze has some strength.

Wind and Water Power

All over the world people have used wind and water power to do useful things.

Huge **hydroelectric dams** use a flow of water to turn the gigantic turbines of generators that produce electricity.

Wind and water power can also be destructive. Rising flood waters can wash out roads and bridges and flood buildings.

The winds of tornados and hurricanes can rip roofs off and destroy houses.

Strong winds can stir up loose particles of sand and dirt into the air.

Springtime snow melt, summer downpours, autumn hurricanes, and winter winds all exert terrific strength that can change the face of the Earth.

Erosion

Erosion is the result of wind and water wearing away the land. It can happen suddenly, overnight, or slowly, over millions of years.

Some beautiful and unusual **landforms** are the result of erosion by wind and water.

Erosion, whether by wind or water, is a force that can move mountains. Piece, by tiny piece, erosion slowly changes the shape of the mountain.

The eroded particles may be carried for miles before they are **deposited**. They may become part of a sand dune in a desert far away. Or they may be washed into the ocean to become part of an offshore **barrier** island.

People, plants, and animals are all affected by the changes that erosion brings. **Ecosystems** may be ruined when plants die as the soil is carried away or is covered by deposits of eroded material.

Animals and people cannot survive in the ruined **environment** and may have to leave as the land is changed.

Weather Changes

Climate and weather changes also occur as the land changes. Have you noticed how much cooler it is in a forest than in an open field with no trees for shade?

When plants are unable to live and create shade in an eroded place, the ground heats up. Then the soil dries up, creating a desert.

The next time it's raining hard or the wind is howling, take a look around and notice what changes are happening. You may be surprised to see how much stuff is floating or flying away. And how much stuff gets left behind!

Glossary

barrier (BA ree ur) — something, like a wall, that protects

deposited (di POZ uh ted) — to place, lay down, or leave behind

ecosystem (EE koh siss tuhm) — a community of plants, animals, and other living things that depend on each other.

environment (en VYE ruhn muhnt) — the natural world of the land, sea, and air

erosion (i ROH zhuhn) — the gradual wearing away of soil or rock by water or wind

hydroelectric dam (hye droh i LEK trik DAM) — a barrier that holds back water to make electricity

landform (LAND form) — a part of the Earth shaped by erosion or other movement

particle (PAR tuh kuhl) — a very small piece of something

Index

Further Reading

Bailey, Jacqui. *Cracking Up: A Story About Erosion*. Picture Window Books, 2006.
Riley, Joelle. *Erosion*. Lerner, 2007.
Spilsbury, Louise. *Disappearing Mountain and Other Earth Mysteries*. Raintree Publishers, 2006.

Websites to Visit

en.wikipedia.org/wiki/erosion
www.askforkids.com
www.geography4kids.com/map

About the Author

Thomas F. Sheehan is retired from 40 years of teaching elementary, middle, secondary and post-secondary science. He is currently authoring science texts, which speak to children. Sheehan and his wife, Susan, reside on their farm in Mount Chase, Maine.